Chef Ricardo's Caribbean Cuisine Cookbook

www.fast-print.net/store.php

CHEF RICARDO'S CARIBBEAN CUISINE COOKBOOK
Copyright © Chef Ricardo 2015

A catalogue record for this book is available from the British Library

ISBN 978-178035-789-8

First Published 2015 by
Fast-Print Publishing of Peterborough, England.

I do hereby dedicate this book
to my beautiful daughter Kayla

Jamaican cuisine

This Caribbean Cuisine Cookbook has a blend of recipes from the islands using a variety of the wonderful produce, spices and cooking techniques to be found there, which have been influenced by the many different cultures and brought by those who have come from other parts of the world. This diverse cultural influence is still prominent in Caribbean dishes today.

Among the most popular Caribbean dishes are salt fish (codfish) which is the national dish of Jamaica, fried dumplings, curry goat, ackee, fried plantain, jerk chicken, jerk pork, steamed cabbage, rice-and-peas and a wide variety of seafood dishes. Jamaican patties, a type of savoury pastry or turnover, along with other pastries and breads are also traditionally produced as are delicious fruit drinks and, of course, the famous Jamaican rum.

The popularity and influence of Jamaican cuisine has expanded as people emigrated from the island to further their horizons, especially during the 20th century.

With not a limp lettuce leaf in sight, this creative selection of recipes will convert even the most wary salad eaters. Each dish is full of imaginative ingredients, beautifully arranged with the tastiest of dressings.

Grouped so that you can choose your ingredients season by season, you will find that whilst many of the salads make impressive main dishes, others can also be enjoyed as starters or as exquisite accompaniments. Chef Ricardo is a great salad lover and an advocate for eating good healthy food.

When time is short, or when you want something fresh and crisp to eat, Chef Ricardo's book will provide you with ideas for snack meals and for salads ranging from the most simple to elaborate main dish salads. As a bonus Chef Ricardo offers useful advice on preparation and serving. Every recipe is illustrated in colour.

Gone are the days when salads were only served on hot summer days and always consisted of lettuce, tomato and cucumber. Now salads are served all year round and include numerous exciting ingredients, depending on the seasonal food available.

Salads can be served for all sorts of occasions and can range from sustainable main courses to colourful side dishes and sophisticated starters. They may be simple to prepare, requiring only a few minutes to assemble before serving, or they may involve more elaborate preparations in advance. Whichever type of salad you choose, it will always be fun to put together, as salads invariably consist of contrasting flavours, colours and textures.

Contents

JAMAICAN RUM CAKE

Ingredients:

- 2 cups butter
- 2 cups white sugar
- 8 eggs
- ¼ cup white rum (optional)
- 1 tablespoon lime juice
- 1 teaspoon vanilla extract
- 1 tablespoon almond extract
- Grated zest of one lime
- Coconut Gizzada
- 2 pounds chopped dried mixed fruit
- 2 cups red wine
- 1 cup dark molasses
- 2½ cups all-purpose flour
- 3 teaspoons baking powder
- ½ teaspoon ground nutmeg
- ½ teaspoon ground allspice
- ½ teaspoon ground cinnamon
- 1 pinch salt

Method:

- Preheat oven to gas mark 4. Grease and flour two 9-inch round cake pans.
- In a large bowl, cream together the butter and sugar until light and fluffy. Beat in eggs, then add rum, lime juice, vanilla, almond extract and lime zest. Stir in mixed fruit, wine, and molasses. Sift together flour, baking powder, nutmeg, allspice, cinnamon and salt. Fold into batter, being careful not to over-mix. Pour into prepared pans.
- Bake in preheated oven for 80 to 95 minutes, or until a knife inserted into the centre comes out clean. Let cool in pan for 10 minutes, then turn out onto a wire rack and cool completely.
- For best results, fruits should be soaked in wine for at least four weeks, or boiled in the wine.
- Use a combination of raisins, currants, golden raisins, prunes and dried cherries, or any dried fruit of your preference.
- Additional wine or rum can be brushed onto cake as needed to keep moist.

Serves: 8

Preparation time: 45 minutes

Recipe by Chef Ricardo!

"A dark, rich fruit cake for wine and fruit lovers! This is a recipe I use at Christmas and for birthdays. I prefer to use Jamaican Red Label wine and white rum. But you may use your favourites. ENJOY!"

COCONUT GIZZADA

Ingredients:

- 1 cup water
- 1½ cups grated coconut
- 1½ cups brown sugar
- ¼ tsp. grated nutmeg
- 1oz. butter

Method:

- Boil water and sugar together to make syrup (low heat).
- Add the grated coconut and nutmeg to the syrup.
- Stir the ingredients so it does not thicken. Boil for 15 minutes.
- Add the butter.
- Stir ingredients for another six minutes. Be sure the butter is not visible in the filling.
- Allow the filling to cool.

Ingredients for Pastry:

- 2 cups flour
- Iced water
- 1 tsp. shortening
- 1 tbsp. butter
- ½ tsp. salt

Method:

- Sift flour and salt together. Cut the butter and shortening in to small pieces, add to the flour along with the cold water. Make into pastry (dough).
- Wrap pastry in plastic or foil wrap and put in the fridge for half an hour. Remove and using a rolling pin, roll the pastry on a board to a quarter inch thickness. (Flour the board first).
- Cut circles in the pastry using an 8oz cup/glass. (You can also use a cookie cutter).
- Cut 16 circles from it crimping (pinching) each of the pastry circles to form a casing. They will be holders for the filling. Crimp in a uniform pattern as this will give the decorated effect.
- Place the casings on a greased tray and part-bake in the oven (at gas mark 4) for 15 minutes. Place the pastry on a greased baking sheet. Remove them from the oven and then add the filling to the baked pastry. Bake the gizzadas for another 20 minutes. Remove them from the oven allow to cool for 30 minutes.

Serves: 4

Preparation time: 45 minutes

FISH TEA

Ingredients:

- 2lb whole fish
- 2 litres water
- 4 green bananas
- 1 hot pepper
- 4 scallions
- 5 sprigs of thyme
- 2 cloves of garlic
- 2 potatoes
- 1 teaspoon of salt
- 1 teaspoon of black pepper

Method:

- Wash the fish in water and lemon or lime juice.
- If the fish has scales, remove them by running a knife against the grain of the scales.
- Bring the water to the boil, add the fish then simmer for half an hour.
- Chop the bananas, potatoes, garlic and scallions.
- After half an hour of simmering, strain the fish out of the water.
- Add the green bananas, potatoes, scallions, garlic, pepper (unchopped), salt and black pepper to the fish stock.
- When the fish has cooled, separate the bones from the flesh.
- Add the fish to the stock and simmer for half an hour.

Serves: 6

Preparation time: 45 minutes

Fish Tea – Serve in a bowl! Serve in a bowl!

BEAN SPROUTS WITH HONEY AND SOYA SAUCE

Ingredients:

- 1 kg bean sprouts (washed)
- 4 mixed sweet peppers
- 3 tablespoons of honey
- 3 tablespoons of soya sauce

Method:

- Wash the bean sprouts and sweet pepper
- Place the bean sprouts into a large bowl.
- Cut the sweet peppers in half and remove all the seeds, then slice the sweet peppers into very small pieces.
- Place everything into the bowl and add the rest of the ingredients.
- Mix it up and place it onto a serving tray.

Serves: 6

Preparation time: 20 minutes

Chef tips: you can add more honey and soya sauce if you want it to have more flavour. You can also add carrot and many more different vegetables to the mixture.

JAMAICAN STEW PEAS

Ingredients:

- ½ pound of salt beef
- ½ pound of stew beef
- ½ pound of pig's tail
- 2 scallions
- 1 onion
- 3 cloves of garlic
- 3 sprigs of thyme
- 1 scotch bonnet pepper
- 1 tin of red peas (or two cups of red peas, soaked in water overnight
- 1 tin of coconut milk
- ½ teaspoon of black pepper
- ½ teaspoon of salt
- 5 pimento seeds
- 2 cups of flour

Method:

- Boiling off the salt. Boil salt beef and pig's tail for 30 minutes then drain off the salty water. Then boil salt beef and pig's tail again for 30 minutes and drain off the salty water again.
- Frying the stew beef. Gently fry the stew beef to seal it.
- Chopping the meat. Cut the meat into small pieces.
- Boiling the ingredients. Place the peas, meat and three cups of water in a pot, bring to the boil then let simmer for one hour.

- Chopping the garlic, scallion and onion. Chop the onion, scallion and garlic.
- Making spinners. Make dough by mixing two cups of flour with water. Break off small pieces of dough and roll them in to "spinners".
- Boiling the ingredients. After the peas and meat have simmered for an hour, add the tin of coconut milk, onion, scallion, spinners, garlic, thyme, salt, black pepper, pimento and scotch bonnet (the scotch bonnet should NOT be cut up).
- Cook for an hour then remove the scotch bonnet pepper

Serves: 6

Preparation time: 1½ hours

ROAST BREADFRUIT

Ingredients:

- One breadfruit

Method:

- Removing the stalk. Remove the stalk
- Cooking. Breadfruit should ideally be roasted on an open fire.
- If you do not have a fire to roast your breadfruit on, place in a preheated oven at gas mark 4 for about an hour (until the skin has turned brown).
- Slicing. Cut slices from the breadfruit.
- Peeling. Peel the skin and core away from the breadfruit slices.
- Serving. Serve with a breakfast dish such as ackee and salt fish or jerk chicken, okra and salt fish, callaloo and codfish.

Serves: 9

Preparation time: 50 minutes

JAMAICAN BAKED CHICKEN

Ingredients:

- 4 pieces of chicken – a mixture of thighs and drumsticks.
- 1 teaspoon of chicken seasoning
- 1 teaspoon all-purpose
- 1 teaspoon of paprika
- 1 teaspoon of garlic powder
- Pinch of black pepper
- 1 teaspoon of flavoured seasoning
- 1 teaspoon of olive oil
- Pinch of ginger powder
- 1 whole lemon
- 1 teaspoon of chilli powder

Method:

- Put the chicken into a bowl and wash it with the lemon.
- Drain off the water and add all of your ingredients, including the olive oil, to the chicken, rubbing it up.

- Leave in the fridge for 24 hours.
- After that, place it into a baking tray.
- Preheat oven to gas mark 5 and when you start cooking, change it to gas mark 6.

Serves: 4

Preparation time: 45 minutes

Chef tips: You can have baked chicken with rice and peas, white rice, Jamaican dumpling, yam, banana, boiled cassava and boiled breadfruit

JAMAICAN RICE AND PEAS

Ingredients:

- 1 can kidney beans/red peas
- 100g frozen mixed vegetables
- 200g basmati rice, uncooked
- 2 sprigs of fresh thyme
- 20g coconut cream
- 1 bay leaf 1 spring onion
- 1 teaspoon cumin powder
- 1 clove garlic, finely chopped
- ½ teaspoon all-purpose seasoning
- 1 red pepper, de-seeded and diced
- 600ml water

Method:

- Put the beans in a large pan, which has a tight fitting lid, and add water. Then add all the other ingredients, except the rice, and bring to the boil.
- Rinse the rice in warm water before adding to the pot. Stir well.
- Cover the pan and simmer for a further 20-30 minutes or until all the liquid has been absorbed and the rice is cooked. You may need to add more liquid to soften the rice.

Serves: 8

Preparation time: 10 minutes

Cooking time: 30 minutes

CARIBBEAN STEAMED SNAPPER

Ingredients:

- 4 snapper fish or other firm white fish of your choice e.g. coley or cod
- 200g pumpkin, peeled and cubed
- 150g okra, washed and trimmed
- 2 cloves of garlic, crushed
- 2 sweet peppers
- 1 onion, thinly sliced
- 1 can chopped tomatoes
- ½ teaspoon coarse black pepper
- 1 teaspoon ground coriander
- 1 bay leaf
- 2 whole pimentos
- 2 sprigs thyme
- Scotch bonnet pepper, finely sliced (optional)

Method:

- Season the fish with the scotch bonnet, garlic, black pepper, bay leaf, ground coriander and thyme. This can be done in advance and left to marinade in the fridge overnight.
- Add the vegetables and a little water to a non-stick pan and heat gently for 5-7 minutes then place the marinated fish on top of the vegetables and cover with a tight fitting lid.
- Simmer on low heat for 20 minutes or until the flesh is cooked all the way through. Serve with boiled yams or plain rice and vegetables of your choice.

Serves: 4

Preparation time: 15 minutes

Cooking time: 25 minutes

HAPPY NEW YEAR ROAST CHICKEN

Ingredients:

- 1 small whole chicken
- 1kg of baby new potatoes
- 1kg of sweet potatoes (remove skin)
- 1 spoon of chicken seasoning
- 1 spoon of all-purpose seasoning
- 1 teaspoon of garlic granules
- 1 teaspoon of coarse black pepper
- 1 teaspoon of hot & spicy seasoning
- 1 teaspoon of everyday seasoning
- 1 teaspoon of smoked Cajun seasoning
- • 1 teaspoon of paprika
- 1 teaspoon of mixed herbs seasoning
- 1 teaspoon of cooking oil
- 1 handful of spring onion (chopped)
- 1 medium onion (chopped)
- 2 small carrots (chopped)
- 1 clove of garlic (crushed)
- A pinch of thyme
- 1 lemon

Method:

- First wash whole chicken with the lemon, then place into a bowl.
- Add all of the ingredients into the bowl except the potatoes and sweet potatoes.
- Rub up the chicken with the seasonings, stuff the garlic, carrots, onion, spring onion and thyme inside the chicken.
- Then place the chicken onto a baking tray.
- Place the potatoes and sweet potatoes around the chicken in the tray.
- Lastly sprinkle herbs and a tablespoon of oil all over the chicken and potatoes and place into the oven on gas mark 6.

Serves: 6

Preparation time: 1hour

Chef tips: This can be served with rice-and-peas, macaroni cheese, plain rice or pumpkin rice or seasoning rice or vegetable rice.

CHERRY TOMATOES WITH BLACK OLIVE

Ingredients:

- 1 kg of cherry tomatoes (cut in half)
- 2 cups of black olive
- 2 teaspoons of olive oil

Method:

- Wash the plum tomatoes in a bowl of cold water.
- Drain off the water and slice the tomatoes into half, then put them into another bowl and add the olives and oil.
- Mix it up and place it in to a serving dish.
- Put it into the fridge for half an hour before serving.

Serves: 4

Preparation time: 15 minutes

Chef tips: you can serve this as a vegetarian salad or have it as a salad dish on its own.

RED ONION AND SWEET PEPPER SALAD

Ingredients:

- 3 mixed sweet peppers (cut up)
- 2 red onions (cut up)
- 2 cucumbers (cut up)
- 1 lettuce (cut up)

Method:

- Firstly wash all the ingredients except the red onion.
- Cut the sweet peppers, red onions and cucumbers in half and remove all the seeds from the sweet pepper.
- Cut the sweet pepper into wedges.
- Remove the skin from the onion then cut the onion, cucumber and lettuce into small wedges.
- Place everything into a large bowl mixes it up and places it into a serving bowl.
- Place it in the fridge for half an hour before serving.

Serves: 4

Preparation time: 15 minutes

Chef tips: You can serve this with many different meals or serve it as a starter.

ROAST VEGETABLE SALAD

Ingredients:

- 2 kg of courgettes (chopped up small)
- 3 sweet peppers (chopped up small)
- 2 red onions (chopped up small)
- Pinch of course grain black pepper
- 3 tablespoons of olive oil

Method:

- Wash the courgette.
- Once cut up, place it into an oven tray and add sweet peppers, oil, onion and black pepper.
- Mix them together and place in the oven for 20 minutes (gas mark 6).

Serves: 4

Preparation time: 20 minutes

Chef tips: You can use all different types of vegetables to roast and use it as a vegetarian dish or with other main meals.

VEGETARIAN SWEET POTATO MASH

Ingredients:

- 3 tablespoons of oil
- Tablespoon of butter
- 3 kgs of sweet potato (cut up)
- 1 teaspoon of salt

Method:

- Wash the potato, remove the skin from the potato, cut it up very small.
- Put water into the pot and place it on the stove (gas mark 6).
- Place potato into the pot, add salt and cook for 20 minutes.
- Then pour the water down the sink and place the potato into a large bowl and add butter and oil.
- Mash the potato using a potato masher until the potato is smooth and lump free.

Serves: 4

Preparation time: 30 minutes

Chef tips: you can have this with tofu, corn, steam vegetables and many different varieties of vegetarian meals

JACKET POTATO WITH TUNA

Ingredients:

- 1 spring onion (chopped up)
- 1 onion (chopped up)
- 2 tablespoons ketchup
- Half cup sweet corn
- 160 grams of tuna
- Teaspoon of black pepper
- Sweet pepper (chopped up)
- 1 kg of potato
- 1 kg cheddar cheese
- 1 large tomato (chopped up)
- 2 tablespoons of olive oil

Method:

- Wash the potato and place into the oven for 20 minutes gas mark 6.
- Place a medium frying pan on the stove, add the oil to the frying pan and heat the oil for three minutes on a medium flame.
- Add all the ingredients except the ketchup, tuna and sweet corn to the frying pan. Fry it for five minutes, add tuna, ketchup and sweet corn to the frying pan and fry it for another 5-10 more minutes then turn off the stove.
- Check the oven to see if the potato is baked, you will know this if the potato looks golden/brown or soft.
- Take out the potato, cut it in half and add the tuna from the frying pan in between the potato. If you want you could place some grated cheese on top

Serves: 4

Preparation time: 45 minutes to an hour

Chef tips: You can place the butter in between the potato when first cut. You can also have this with baked beans, salad or any other side dishes of your choice.

AMERICAN COLESLAW

Ingredients:

- 1 kg cabbage (chopped up fine)
- 1 kg carrot (shredded)
- 1½ cup of raisins
- 1 spoon of sugar
- 450 grams of mayonnaise
- 1 large bowl

Method:

- Grate the cabbage and the carrots and place it into the bowl.
- Then add all the other ingredients, mayonnaise, sugar and only one cup of raisins.
- Mix it all together then place it into another bowl. Add the rest of the raisons on top of it.
- Place the bowl into the fridge for half an hour before eating.

Serves: 4

Preparation time: 30 minutes

Chef tips: You can have this with a wide range of dishes – for example sandwiches, rice and peas, jerk pork, festival dumpling, fried dumpling, fried plantain or jerk chicken.

FRUIT COUSCOUS

Ingredients:

- 1 kg of couscous
- 1 cup of apricot (cut up into small strips)
- 1 cup of mixed dry fruits
- 1 large bowl
- 2 teaspoons of lemon juice
- Pinch of salt
- 1 teaspoon of sugar

Method:

- Place the couscous, salt, sugar and lemon juice into the large bowl
- Add hot water to the couscous, but make sure the water is only a little bit above the couscous.
- Leave the couscous in the bowl for 15 minutes.
- After, check if it is cooked; if it is leave it for half an hour to cool.
- Place the raisons in a small container with hot water for 10 minutes.
- Then pour out the hot water and let it cool for five minutes.
- Cut up the apricot into small strips.
- Add the mixed fruits and the apricot, mix it up and place it into a new bowl.

Serves: 4

Preparation time: 30 minutes

Chef tips: You may add many more ingredients that you like. You can have this as a side dish and other different salads like mixed salad, olive, tomato, cucumber and rocket.

BUTTER POTATO AND RED ONION

Ingredients:

- 1 kg potato (cooked)
- 2 red onions (chopped up fine)
- 3 tablespoons of butter
- 2 spoons of olive oil
- Pinch of salt
- 1 teaspoon of sugar

Method:

- Put hot water into a pot and place it onto the stove, gas mark 6.
- Remove the skin from the potato and wash it. Cut the potato into four then place it into the pot with salt.
- Leave it to cook for 20 minutes.
- Then add the butter and let it cook for another five minutes.
- Check if the potato is cooked; if cooked pour out the water.
- Fry the onion for 10 minutes and add sugar to the onion.
- When the onion is fried, put the onion with the potato.
- Place everything into a large bowl.

Serves: 5

Preparation time: 20 minutes

Chef tips: You can have this with ackee and salt fish, steam callaloo and stir-fry vegetables.

BASIL PASTA SALAD

Ingredients:

- 1 kg pasta
- 400 grams of tomato sauce
- 1 teaspoon of salt
- 1 handful of spring onions
- 1 teaspoon of sugar
- 1 teaspoon of mixed herb
- 1 handful of basil
- 3 spoons of olive oil

Method:

- Put water into a pot and place the pot onto the stove on a high flame to get hot.
- Once hot, add the pasta, olive oil and salt. Stir it and leave it to cook for 15 minutes.
- Once cooked, strain out the water and run some cold water on it. When the pasta is cooled place it into a large bowl.
- Place the tomato sauce into a pot and make it hot for 15 minutes. Chop up the basil and mixed herb and add it to the sauce along with the sugar. Leave it for 10 minutes.
- After 10 minutes take it of the stove and leave it to cool for 10 minutes. Once cooled add it to the pasta and mix it up and place it into another serving dish. Sprinkle the spring onion onto of the pasta.

Serves: 6

Preparation time: 45 minutes

LEMON CHICKEN SALAD

Ingredients:

- 1 kg of chicken breasts (cooked)
- 3 sweet peppers (chopped up)
- 2 large cucumbers (chopped up)
- 1 teaspoon of paprika
- 3 tablespoons of lemon juice
- 3 tablespoons of olive oil
- Handful coriander (chopped up)
- 1 teaspoon of coarse black pepper
- Handful of spring onion (chopped up)

Method:

- Put water into a medium size pot and place it onto the stove.
- Place the chicken into the pot and boil the chicken for 15 minutes.
- After, take it out and leave it to cool down; once cooled down cut up the chicken into small sized pieces
- Add all the ingredients into the bowl with the chicken and mix them together.
- If you want, you could add more oil, lemon juice and paprika.
- Place the bowl in the fridge for 20 minutes.

Serves: 5

Preparation time: 30 minutes

BROCCOLI SALAD

Ingredients:

- 1 kg broccoli (cooked)
- 2 red sweet peppers (chopped up very small)
- 1 teaspoon of black pepper
- 2 spoons of olive oil
- 1 teaspoon of blended garlic

Method:

- Put a small amount of water into a medium size pot.
- Place the broccoli inside the pot and boil it for 15 minutes.
- Once cooked strain out the water and leave the broccoli to cool down.
- When cooled, place the broccoli into a small bowl then add all the other ingredients rub them together.
- Put cling film around the whole bowl and place bowl into the fridge for 20 minutes.

Serves: 4

Preparation time: 20 minutes

Chef tips: You can have this with many different meals like Jamaican rice and peas, jerk chicken, fried fish, jerk pork and other foods like that.

MIX UP SALAD

Ingredients:

- 1 kg rocket (washed)
- 1 kg of spinach (washed)
- 1 kg of lettuce (washed)
- 2 red sweet peppers (cut up)
- 2 kgs of tomatoes

Method:

- After you have washed all the ingredients place them into a medium bowl except the tomatoes and sweet peppers.
- Remove the seat from the tomato and pepper.
- Slice them both up small and add it to the rest of the ingredients in the bowl and mix it up.
- Place it into the fridge for 20 minutes.

Serves: 4

Preparation time: 20 minutes

Chef tips: you can also add olive oil, lemon juice, and more vegetables like cucumber, shredded carrot, cabbage or sweetcorn. You can have this salad as a side dish with French dressing on top of the salad.

CHEESE SALAD

Ingredients:

- 50 g mayonnaise
- 3 tomatoes
- ½ cup cheese, grated
- ¼ teaspoon black pepper to taste
- 1 onion
- 2 spring onions

Method:

- Mix mayonnaise and cheese with into ball
- Cut tomatoes, onions and spring onions
- Put in to the balls write mayonnaise and cheese and mix it up
- Put it in to refrigerate for 15 minutes
- Serve with lettuce and cucumbers

Serves: 5

Preparation time: 20 minutes

POTATO SALAD

Ingredients:

- 1 kg new potatoes
- 1 red onion (chopped up fine)
- Handful of spring onion (chopped up small)
- 240g mayonnaise
- 1 teaspoon of black pepper
- 3 mixed sweet peppers (chopped up fine)
- Pinch parsley (chopped up fine)

Method:

- Put some water into a pot and place it onto the stove.
- Place the potato into the pot and cook it for 20 minutes, gas mark 6.
- When cooked, drain the water and place the potato into a large bowl and let it cool for 30 minutes.
- Add the rest of the ingredients into the bowl and mix it up together, then place it into a serving bowl.
- Put the bowl into the fridge for 30 minutes before serving.

Serves: 4

Preparation time: 1 hour

VEGETARIAN BEEF TOMATO SALAD

Ingredients:

- 1 large beef tomato
- 1 kg of lettuce
- 1 ice cream scoop spoon

Method:

- Wash the beef tomato and lettuce.
- Cut the beef tomato into half and using the ice cream scoop spoon, scoop out the inside of the tomato.
- Cut the lettuce into chunky pieces and stuff it inside the beef tomato.
- Place it on a serving plate and put it in the fridge for 15 minutes to cool before serving.

Serves: 1

Preparation time: 15 minutes

Chef tips: with the beef tomato you can add more ingredients like olive oil, olives, a pinch of pepper, lemon chilli and mint dressing, rosemary and red pepper dressing, fennel and lime, French dressing, cheddar cheese and many varieties of ingredients. Or you could just have it on its own, as a vegetarian or diet meal.

HONEY COURGETTE

Ingredients:

- 2 kg of courgettes (cut in round pieces)
- 4 tablespoons honey
- Pinch of coarse grain black pepper
- 2 teaspoons olive oil
- Pinch of salt

Method:

- Put the courgettes into pot of water and place it on to the stove.
- Cook it for 15 minutes, gas mark 6.
- Add all ingredients except honey and pepper.
- After the courgettes are cooked, strain off the water and place it into a bowl.
- Put the honey and black pepper into the bowl and mix it up.
- Place it all into a serving bowl and leave it to cool for 15 minutes before serving.

Serves: 4

Preparation time: 25 minutes

Chef tips: this is a beautiful recipe from Chef Ricardo. You can have it as a vegetarian meal. You can serve it cold or warm.

OLIVE OIL WITH ROAST PEPPER AND SPINACH

Ingredients:

- 6 mixed peppers
- 1 kg spinach
- 2 tablespoons of olive oil

Method:

- Wash the sweet peppers, cut them into small diced pieces and place on an oven tray.
- Add the olive oil to the sweet peppers and rub them together.
- Put the tray into oven for 20 minutes gas mark 6.
- When cooked leave it to cool down for 20 minutes.
- Wash off the spinach and let it drain off for 20 minutes.
- Once drained, place the spinach on a serving tray, then put the sweet pepper on top the spinach before serving.

Serves: 6

Preparation time: 45 minutes

Chef tips: This is a beautiful dish with olive oil, peppers and spinach. You can also have this with many different meals, especially vegetarian dishes.

VEGETARIAN CABBAGE SOUP

Ingredients:

- 1 kg cabbage (washed and cut up small)
- 1 clove garlic (cut up fine)
- 1 small onion (cut up fine)
- 1 spring onion (cut up fine)
- 1 bunch of thyme (cut up fine)
- 1 carrot (cut up fine)
- 1 irish potato (cut up fine)
- 4 cups of water
- 1 teaspoon olive oil

Method:

- Place a medium pot on the stove with the olive oil and heat it for 10 minutes gas mark 6.
- Cut up the potato, onion, garlic, spring onion, carrot and cabbage into small pieces.
- Add all the ingredients into the pot and mix it up. Cook it for 15 minutes.
- Take some of the cabbage out and put it into a small bowl and add the rest of the water to the pot, cook it for another 15 minutes.
- Once cooked use a hand blender and blend it until gets a ceramic look. When blending add a little bit of water to the pot. Let it cook or another 10 minutes.
- When cooked place it into a serving bowl and put the rest of the cabbage on top of the soup in the bowl.

Serves: 4

Preparation time: 1 hour

Chef tips: You can add as many different vegetables to the soup as you like. You can also have croutons with the soup; the croutons must be whole wheat bread.

CROUTONS FOR SOUP

Ingredients:

- 1 kg bread
- 3 tablespoons of olive oil
- 3 spoons of mixed dry herbs
- 2 spoons of Cajun seasoning
- 1 spoon of coarse black pepper

Method:

- Cut the bread into squares and place it into a large bowl.
- Add all the ingredients to the bowl, mix it up.
- Put a sheet of greased paper onto the oven tray.
- Put all the mixture onto the tray and place the tray into the oven for 30 minutes until it gets brown and crispy (gas mark 6).
- When it gets brown and crispy, take it out of the oven and leave it to cool for 10 minutes.
- Place it into a serving bowl.

Serves: 4

Preparation time: 45 minutes

Chef tips: You can have this by itself or with soup, chicken salad and many different kinds of salads that you like to eat.

CHEESE AND BEEF TOMATO SANDWICH

Ingredients:

- 1 loaf of bread
- 1 kg of grated cheese
- 1 kg tomatoes
- 1 spoon of butter

Method:

- Wash the tomatoes, slice them into small pieces and cut them in half.
- Spread butter on each of the bread slices, add the cheese and tomato on top of the sliced bread and cover it with another slice.
- Cut into four pieces and place on a serving plate

Serves: 4

Preparation time 15 minutes

Chef tips: You can mix the tomato and cheese with mayonnaise before adding it to the bread.

COLESLAW SANDWICH

Ingredients:

- 1 kg cabbage
- 1 kg carrots (grated)
- 1 loaf of bread
- 240g of mayonnaise
- 1 teaspoon of sugar
- Pinch of coarse grain black pepper
- 1 small onion

Method:

- Grate the cabbage and the carrots and place it into the bowl.
- Add the mayonnaise, sugar, onion and black pepper.
- Mix it all together then place it into another bowl.
- Get one slice of bread and spread the coleslaw on it, cover the slice of bread with another slice and then cut it into four pieces.
- Place it on a serving plate.

Serves: 4

Preparation time: 25-30 minutes

Chef tips: You can add all different ingredients to you coleslaw mixture, like spring onion; you can add butter to the bread first.

MIXED FRUIT BOWL

Ingredients:

- 1 cantaloupe melon
- 1 water melon
- 1 honey dew melon
- 2 oranges
- 3 green apples
- 3 red apples
- 1 large cup of grapes (red and green)
- 1 cup of strawberries
- 2 cups orange juice
- 1 cup of apple juice

Method:

- Wash all the fruit, peel them (except the strawberries and grapes), cut them up very small, and place them into a large bowl
- Add strawberries, grapes and orange juice. Mix it up with a tablespoon
- Cover with cling film and place it in your fridge for 20 minutes

Serves: 4

Preparation time: 20 minutes

Chef tips: You can also add many varieties of fruits that you like. You can add fresh mint and red syrup. You can also have it with yoghurt and ice cream.

SWEET CHILLI CHICKEN

Ingredients:

- 1 kg chicken breast
- 1 teaspoon of paprika
- 240g sweet chilli sauce
- 1 teaspoon coarse black pepper
- 1 spoon of chicken seasoning
- 1 spoon of all-purpose seasoning
- 1 spoon of oil
- 1 spoon of Cajun seasoning

Method:

- Wash the chicken and place it into a large bowl.
- Add all the other ingredients except the sweet chilli sauce and mix it up.
- Put the chicken on an oven tray and place it in the oven for 25 minutes, gas mark 6.
- Once the chicken is cooked, cool it down for 20 minutes.
- When cooled, cut the chicken into small strips or you can tear it with your hands.
- Once you have done that place it into a large bowl.
- Add the sweet chilli sauce to the bowl, mix it up and place it into a serving bowl.

Serves: 5

Preparation time: 45 minutes

Chef tips: You can have this with different kinds of salad like rice salad, rocket salad, spinach salad, mixed leaf salad and many more salads that you enjoy eating. You can also leave the chicken seasoned for 24 hours before baking.

CHICKEN SALAD

Ingredients:

- 1 kg chicken breast
- 1 kg lettuce
- 1 spoon of oil
- 1 spoon Cajun seasoning
- 2 red peppers
- 242g of salad cream
- Pinch of coarse black pepper

Method:

- Wash the chicken breast and place it into a bowl, seasoning it with Cajun seasoning, black pepper and oil.
- Place it into the oven for 20 minutes, gas mark 6.
- When cooked take it out and leave it to cool for 30 minutes.
- After, cut the chicken breast small pieces and put into a large bowl.
- Wash off the lettuce and the sweet peppers, cut them up small and add them to the bowl with the chicken.
- Add the salad cream to the bowl and mix it up.
- Place it into a serving bowl and put into a fridge for 20 minutes before serving.

Serves: 6

Preparation time: 30 minutes

Chef tips: You can add more ingredients to eat like a pinch of sugar and more mixed leaves.

HONEY CHICKEN

Ingredients:

- 1 kg of chicken thigh
- 1 teaspoon Cajun seasoning
- 1 teaspoon paprika
- 1 teaspoon of all-purpose seasoning
- 1 teaspoon of chicken seasoning
- 1 spoon of oil
- 1 pinch of black pepper
- 4 tablespoons of honey
- 4 large tomatoes
- 3 mixed peppers
- Pinch of parsley

Method:

- Wash the chicken thigh and place it into a large bowl with all the other ingredients, except the tomato, peppers and parsley.
- Mix it up and put it into an oven tray and place it into the oven, gas mark 6.
- Wash the tomato and peppers, dice them into small pieces and place them into a bowl, mixing them up.
- Once the chicken is cooked, place it on a serving plate and add the tomatoes and peppers on top of the chicken.
- Sprinkle the parsley on the top of the chicken before serving.
- You can also leave the chicken seasoned for 24 hours before baking.

Serves: 5

Preparation time: 45 minutes

Chef tips: You can have this with a variety of meals like rice and peas, plain rice, pumpkin rice, callaloo rice and many more different types of dishes.

JERK CHICKEN

Ingredients:

- 8 chicken legs
- 1 teaspoon Caribbean Jerk sauce
- 2 spring onions (chopped up fine)
- 1 teaspoon all-purpose seasoning
- 1 teaspoon black pepper
- Salt if needed
- Thyme (chopped up fine)
- 1 onion (chopped up fine)
- 3 cloves garlic (chopped up fine)

Method:

- Wash chicken thighs, then add salt, black pepper, jerk sauce, chopped spring onion, crushed or thinly sliced garlic, and all-purpose seasoning.
- Rub all the seasoning into the chicken, cover and leave to marinate for 20-30 minutes.
- After the chicken has been left to marinate for this time place on tray and cook for 30-40 minutes.

Serves: 8

Preparation time: 1 hour

Chef tips: You can serve this with festival dumpling, fired dumplings, rice-and-peas, plain rice or salad.

ACKEE/SALT FISH

Ingredients:

- 1 Can of ackee, drained
- 1 kg boneless salt cod
- 3 tablespoons olive oil
- 2 onions, chopped up fine
- 1 pinch of thyme
- ¼ scotch bonnet pepper skin ,finely chopped up
- 1 small tomato, chopped
- 3 mixed sweet peppers, chopped up
- 1 teaspoon black pepper
- 1 white onion chopped up
- 2 stalk spring onions chopped up

Method:

- Soak the salt cod in a pot of water overnight to remove most of the salt. If the cod is still very salty, boil in water for 20 minutes.
- Drain cod and cut or break into small pieces.
- Heat oil in a frying pan. Add the onions, thyme, scotch bonnet pepper, tomato and green peppers. Stir for a few minutes.
- Add the cod. Stir.
- Simmer for 5-7 minutes, and then add the can of drained ackee.
- Do not stir because this will cause the ackee to break up.
- Cook for a few more minutes then sprinkle with black pepper.
- Place into a serving bowl.

Serves: 4

Preparation time: 30 mintues

Chef tips: Ackee and salt fish is Jamaica's national dish. You can have this with a wide variety of dishes like roast bread fruit, fried dumpling, hard food, boiled banana and many more Caribbean foods.

SWEET FRIED PLANTAIN

Ingredients:

- Three plantains
- 1 cup of oil

Method:

- First, heat the oil in a frying pan for 10 seconds.
- Then peel the plantains and cut them up into small pieces
- Place plantains in frying pan, until both sides of plantain are brown
- After browned, take the plantain out and place on a plate.

Serves: 4 persons

Preparation time: 20mins

Chef tips: plantain is very sweet and you can have it with a wide range of Caribbean meals.

SWEET CHILLI RICE

Ingredients:

- 3 cups of rice
- 1 medium cup of sweet chilli sauce
- 1 tablespoon of olive oil
- 1 teaspoon of salt
- 3½ cups of water

Method:

- Place the rice into a large bowl and wash it with cold water.
- Pour off the water and put the rice into a medium sized pot.
- Add the water to the rice then place it on the stove, add the rest of the ingredients to the pot then mix it up.
- Cook it for 20 minutes, check if it's cooked and if it's not, leave it to cook for an extra eight minutes.
- Once cooked place it into a serving bowl.

Serves: 8

Preparation time: 30 minutes

Chef tips: you can have this rice with many varieties of meat including bbq chicken, sweet and sour chicken, jerk pork, steamed fish or oxtail.

SWEETCORN RICE

Ingredients:

- 2 cups of basmati rice
- 1 cup of sweetcorn
- 1 teaspoon of salt
- 2½ cups of water
- 1 tablespoon of butter

Method:

- Put a medium pot on the stove and add 2½ cups of water into the pot.
- Wash the rice
- Add all the ingredients
- Let it cook for 20 minutes on low heat.

Serves: 6

Preparation time: 30 minutes

Chef tips: You can have this rice with many varieties of meat including bbq chicken, sweet and sour chicken, jerk pork, steamed fish or oxtail.

HOMEMADE WEDGES

Ingredients:

- 1 kg baking potatoes
- 1 teaspoon Cajun seasoning
- Pinch of coarse grain black pepper
- Pinch of salt
- 2 tablespoons of olive oil

Method:

- Cut the potatoes into wedges and place them in a large bowl of cold water.
- Leave to soak for 30 minutes.
- Then drain off the water and add all of the other ingredients to the bowl of potatoes. Mix it up.
- Put a sheet of greased paper on the tray, place the wedges on the greased paper, and put the tray in the oven for 45 minutes, gas mark 7/160-180 Celsius.
- When cooked place them in a serving dish.

Serves: 4

Preparation time: 1 hour

Chef tips: You can have the wedges with a wide range of meats including steak, chicken, hot wings and bbq ribs.

QUEEN ROAST CHICKEN

Ingredients:

- 1 small whole chicken
- 1kg of baby new potatoes
- 1kg of sweet potatoes (remove skin)
- 1 spoon of chicken seasoning
- 1 spoon of all-purpose seasoning
- 1 teaspoon of garlic granules
- 1 teaspoon of coarse black pepper
- 1 teaspoon of hot & spicy seasoning
- 1 teaspoon of everyday seasoning
- 1 teaspoon of smoked Cajun seasoning
- 1 teaspoon of paprika
- 1 teaspoon of mixed herbs seasoning
- 1 teaspoon of cooking oil
- 1 handful of spring onion (chopped)
- 1 medium onion (chopped)
- 2 small carrots (chopped)
- 1 clove of garlic (crushed)
- A pinch of thyme
- 1 lemon

Method:

- Wash whole chicken with the lemon, then place into a bowl
- Add all of the ingredients into the bowl except the potatoes and sweet potatoes
- Rub the chicken with the seasoning, stuff the garlic, carrots, onion, spring onion and the thyme inside the chicken
- Place the chicken onto a baking tray
- Place the potatoes and sweet potatoes around the chicken in the tray
- Lastly sprinkle herbs and a tablespoon of oil all over the chicken and potatoes and place into oven on gas mark 6.

Serves: 6

Preparation time: 1 hour

Chef tips: This can be served with rice–and-peas, macaroni cheese, plain rice, pumpkin rice, seasoning rice or vegetables

CHEF RICARDO'S SPECIAL CORNED BEEF

Ingredients:

- 340g of corned beef
- 1 cup of sweetcorn
- 1 large onion (chopped)
- A handful of spring onion (chopped)
- Mixed sweet peppers (chopped)
- A pinch of thyme
- A pinch of black pepper
- ½ cup of shredded carrots
- 1 teaspoon of all-purpose seasoning
- 1 teaspoon of everyday seasoning
- 3 tablespoons of tomato ketchup
- 1 teaspoon of hot pepper sauce
- A pinch of scotch bonnet pepper
- 3 tablespoons of oil
- 2 tomatoes (cut up small)

Method:

- Place oil into the frying pan on the stove at gas mark 4
- Place corned beef into a small bowl, put into the microwave. After hot, take it out and mash with a fork
- Place all the ingredients, apart from the corned beef and tomato ketchup, into a frying pan and cook for 10 minutes, continuing to stir it
- Then add the corned beef and ketchup and mix up everything together
- Leave to slowly cook for 5-10 minutes

Serves: 4

Preparation time: 30mins

Chef tips: Serve with plain rice, fried dumpling or hard food. Can add cabbage to corned beef if wanted.

SALT FISH FRITTERS

Ingredients:

- 1 cup of plain flour
- 300 grams of salt fish
- ½ of an onion
- ½- small scotch bonnet pepper
- 1 spring onion
- Half a teaspoon of black pepper
- 1 cup of olive oil
- 1 cup of water

Method:

- Put the salt fish into a pot with water on the stove to boil for 15 minutes. Drain the water from the salt fish and run a little bit of cold water over the salt fish. Then get a large bowl and put the plain flour into it.
- Break the salt fish into small pieces then add it to the flour. Cut the spring onion and onion into small pieces and add it to the flour. Cut a piece of the scotch bonnet pepper (for a hotter flavour use more as desired) and add it to the flour with the black pepper.
- Add a cup of water slowly to the flour and mix until it becomes a soft consistency which runs of the spoon. Taste it to see if it needs salt and if needed, add a pinch.
- Put a frying pan on the stove gas mark 5 and add the oil to it until it gets heated. Use a teaspoon to take small spoonfuls from the bowl and drop it into the frying pan, three at a time depending on the size of your frying pan. Fry for three minutes and when brown turn it over to the other side and fry for a further three minutes.
- Following this, break one in half and check if it is cooked. (Fritter should not look pasty.)

Serves: 6

Preparation time: 30 minutes

Chef tips: Why not try this like a Jamaican breakfast with Jamaican hard bread and mint tea?

HOME-MADE FRIED DUMPLING

Ingredients:

- 2 cups of self raising flour
- 1 teaspoon of salt
- 1 cup of milk
- 1 tablespoon of butter
- 2 cups of sunflower oil
- 1 teaspoon sugar

Method:

- Place the flour in a mixing bowl; add salt, sugar and butter binding it together with the milk slowly.
- When this is done, knead the mixture in the bowl.
- When the mixture has been kneaded into dough, break small amounts at a time and knead again in the palm of your hands into a round shape and press flat.
- Heat the oil in a frying pan and place approximately four pieces (more or less depending on the size of your pan) into the pan making sure that the oil is not too hot or the dumplings will burn.
- Fry on each side for 5-6 minutes then continue with the remaining dough.
- Place kitchen paper into a bowl before taking dumplings out of the pan to get rid of excess oil.

Serves: 4

Preparation time: 30 minutes

Chef tips: Make the dumpling mixture, cover with cling film and keep in the fridge for 24 hours prior to frying for a softer, moister dumpling.

CUISINE CHICKEN SOUP

Ingredients:

- 2 leg quarters of chicken
- 2 cups of flour
- 1 cup of cornmeal
- ¼ pumpkin
- 2 large irish potatoes
- 2 large carrots
- 2 large sweet potatoes
- 2 spring onions
- 2 onions
- 1 hot pepper
- 1 ripe plantain
- 1 gram of yam
- 1 christophene
- ½ breadfruit
- 2 packets cock soup
- 2 teaspoon of salt
- A pinch of thyme
- ¼ teaspoon of pimento

Method:

- Place a medium sized pot of water on the stove. Cut up the pumpkin and add to the water.
- Wash the chicken, cut it up and add it to the water, get a clean bowl and add flour and cornmeal to the bowl.
- Add half a teaspoon of salt with one cup of cold water to the bowl, little by little until it turns into dough.
- Then you take piece by piece and make them into dumplings.
- Then you add the rest of the hard ingredients and let it cook for 15 minutes
- Then add the onion, thyme, cock soup, pepper, pimento, salt and spring onion.
- Lastly let it simmer for 15 minutes then taste.

Serves: 6

Preparation time: Half an hour

Total time: 1 hour

CHEF RICARDO'S MACARONI CHEESE

Ingredients:

- 1kg of boiled macaroni
- 520g of cheddar cheese (strong mature)
- 1 pint of milk
- 250g of butter
- 1 cup of plain flour
- 1 small cup of sweetcorn
- A pinch of coarse black pepper

Method:

- Pour the milk into a medium pot and place on stove at gas mark 4, slowly warming the milk
- After the milk is hot add the butter and flour and blend with hand mixer until thick and creamy
- Add only 250g of the cheese into the pot and continue to mix until thick and smooth
- Lastly add the rest of the ingredients into the pot and stir
- After you boil the macaroni add the sauce and mix it up
- Place it into a baking bowl
- Sprinkle the remaining cheese on top of the macaroni
- Place into oven, slow cooking on gas mark 5 until the top browns.

Serves: 5

Preparation time: 45 minutes

Chef tips: Can add a teaspoon of sugar if wanted, can use sweet pepper, onion, cooked bacon pieces, or spring onion if wanted. My idea is to serve barbeque chicken with the macaroni and cheese, the best dish in the world.

CHEF RICARDO'S JERK PORK

Ingredients:

- 1kg of jerk pork
- 2 spoonfuls of jerk seasoning
- 2 large onions (remove skin and chop up)
- A bunch of spring onions (chopped)
- 2 cloves of garlic
- 2 spoonfuls of all-purpose seasoning
- 1 teaspoon of coarse black pepper
- 1 teaspoon of everyday seasoning
- 4 carrots (chopped up)
- 2 big tablespoons of browning sauce
- A pinch of thyme
- 2 scotch bonnet peppers (cut in half)
- 4 pints of water
- 2 lemons

Method:

- First wash the meat with the lemons, the place into a large bowl
- Add all the ingredients into the bowl and mix with the meat
- Put to soak for 24 hours
- After 24 hours place into a pot and add the 4 pints of water
- Taste to see if needs salt or more jerk seasoning
- Place on stove on gas mark 6
- Cook it for 25 minutes. If not cooked add boiled water from the kettle and cook until soft
- Lastly place into a baking tray and put into the oven for 15-20 minutes

Serves: 4

Preparation time: 1 hour 20 minutes

Chef tips: You can jerk the meat on a grill or place into the oven with foil over it if wanted but the easy way is to cook it in the oven. Serve with plain rice, dumpling or festival dumpling.

BROWN STEW CHICKEN

Ingredients:

- 2 onions – sliced
- 1 spring onion – chopped
- 4 tablespoons browning
- Sweet chilli sauce
- 2 pegs of garlic
- Ground black pepper
- 3 sweet peppers
- 2 tomatoes
- ¼ teaspoon of salt
- Ketchup
- Thyme
- Chop and wash (1) chicken leg and thighs
- 1 teaspoon all-purpose seasoning
- 2 carrots
- 2 potatoes

Method:

- Wash, remove skin and chop chicken into small pieces.
- After doing this add black pepper, onions, spring onion, browning, sweet chilli sauce, thyme, ketchup and garlic.
- After doing this rub in the mixture and leave to marinate for 20-30 minutes.
- Heat the pot that you desire to use and add 2 tablespoons of oil.
- After doing this throw the chicken and the seasoning into the pot.
- Stir so that the meat will not stick.
- After doing this for a period of 5 minutes, cover the pot and leave to cook for 15 minutes, then open again and stir, add two cups of water and leave to simmer for another 15 minutes.

Serves: 4

Preparation time: 45 minutes

Chef tips: This is best served with plain white rice or rice and peas.

JAMAICA JERK FISH

Ingredients:

- 4 snapper fish (or any fish of your choice)
- 1 teaspoon ground black pepper
- 1 teaspoon fish seasoning
- 2 teaspoon jerk seasoning

Method:

- Wash the fish in vinegar and make sure that it has been properly cleaned.
- Pre-heat the oven at gas mark 5.
- Season the fish with black pepper, salt and fish seasoning.
- Add 2 tablespoons of jerk seasoning to the fish.
- After the fish has been prepared, line the baking dish with kitchen foil, then place the fish on top and cover with another piece of foil.
- Place in the oven and cook for 10-15 minutes on each side.

Serves: 4

Preparation time: 20 minutes

Chef tips: Can be eaten with rice or Jamaican hard-dough bread.

CARIBBEAN POTATO SALAD

Ingredients:

- 4 cups of cooked potato
- ¼ cup of chopped onion
- ¼ cup of red onion
- 2 carrots cut in small dices
- 2 spring onions, cut up
- ¼ teaspoon of black pepper
- ½ cup of mayonnaise
- 2 boiled egg

Method:

- Peel potatoes and then cut them up into dices, put them in a small pot with water and cook for 15 minutes.
- When finished cooking, throw off the water and leave to cool for 10 minutes, then add both onions including the spring onions, carrot, black pepper, mayonnaise and eggs.
- When eggs have finished cooking, put to cool in cold water, remove the shells of the eggs, then cut them up into pieces and add them to the potatoes.
- When done, mix up everything into a large bowl and leave to cool for 20 minutes.

Serves: 6

Preparation time: 45 minutes

LEMON JUICE DRINK

Ingredients:

- 1 cup of white or brown sugar
- 6 lemons
- 3 litre bottle of water
- One large bowl

Method:

- Add the water into a large bowl then pour the sugar into the bowl.
- Cut the lemons in half and squeeze them into a strainer over the bowl and mix it until you can't see the sugar.
- Taste it to see if it needs sugar; if it does add some.

Serves: 6

Preparation time: 15 minutes

Chef tips: You can have this with your Sunday dinner. Also you can add some ice.

GUINNESS PUNCH

Ingredients:

- 3 cans/bottles of Guinness
- 3 tins of Nurishment
- Vanilla essence
- Nutmeg
- 1 tin condensed milk
- Rum (optional)
- Honey (optional)
- Ice (optional)

Method:

- Pour the Guinness into a large jug
- Add the Nurishment
- Add the condensed milk to desired sweetness
- Add spices
- Mix together and taste
- Add optional ingredients if desired
- Place in the fridge and serve cool in a glass with ice.

Serves: approximately six

Preparation time: 15-25 minutes

FRIED GREEN PLANTAIN

Ingredients:

- 1 plantain
- ½ a cup of oil
- 2 cups of water
- 1 teaspoon of salt

Method:

- Get a small bowl and put the two cups of water inside it.
- Put the teaspoon of salt in the water, remove the skin from the plantain, cut it into three and place into the water.
- Leave to soak in the water for 10 minutes.
- Place a frying pan on the stove, put the oil in it and heat for three minutes on a medium heat.
- Take the plantain from the water and put it in the frying pan. While it's frying keep turning the plantain and fry it for six minutes.
- Once fried, put the plantain on a napkin. With another napkin, squeeze the plantain down so it's flat and put it back into the frying pan for three minutes each side.

Serves: 3

Preparation time: 15 minutes

Chef tip: this can go with Jamaican hot chocolate, fry up salt fish, fry up salt mackerel, this is a Jamaican dish.

BEETROOT DRINK

Ingredients:

- 1 pack of beetroot
- 1 tangerine
- 1 orange
- 1 handful of black and white grapes
- 1 handful of strawberries
- 2 cups of water

Method:

- Make sure you wash all the fruit first
- Slice the beetroot, peel the orange,
  peel the tangerine and cut them up into small pieces, then put the fruit into a blender with two cups of water.
- Blend for 10 minutes, and then pour it out with ice.

Preparation time: 20 minutes

Serves: 2

Chef tip: This is a nice drink for summer or for a special occasion. This is a natural drink, with plenty of vitamins so it's healthy.

SWEET POTATO SOUP

Ingredients:

- 1 kilo of sweet potato
- 1 large white onion
- 1 large teaspoon of unsalted butter
- 2 stalks of spring onion
- A pinch of fresh thyme
- A pinch of coarse black pepper
- 3 cloves of garlic
- 1 scotch bonnet pepper
- 3 cups of water

Method:

- Place a medium sized pot on the stove, add the butter to the pot, remove the skin from the sweet potatoes, dice them and add them to the pot.
- Apart from the scotch bonnet pepper, cut up the rest of the ingredients and add them to the pot.
- Cook on a medium heat for 10 minutes, then add the three cups of water and cook for an extra eight minutes until it gets soft.
- Once the mixture's soft put it in a blender and blend it for 10 minutes until it gets smooth.
- Pour it back inside the pot and cook it for five more minutes, then you can serve it.
- Once in a bowl, place the scotch bonnet pepper on top.

Serves: 4

Preparation time: 30 minutes

Chef tip: sweet potato soup is a very healthy soup and it is good for an evening meal.

PAN FRY JERK FISH

Ingredients:

- 1 kilo of haddock, cut into half
- 1 large carrot
- 1 large white onion
- ¼ of each mixed pepper
- A pinch of coarse black pepper
- 1 lemon
- Stalk of spring onion
- Spoon of jerk seasoning
- Pinch of fresh thyme
- 1 clove of garlic
- Half a cup of oil
- 1 spoon of oil

Method:

- Wash the fish, place it in a bowl, add the jerk seasoning and rub it in.
- Put a frying pan on the stove, gas mark 5.
- Put the fish in the frying pan and cook it for three minutes each side until it gets slightly dark golden.
- Place it on a serving tray.
- Get another frying pan, put a spoon of oil in the frying pan and heat it for three minutes.
- Remove the skin from the carrot and cut it up into small wedges with the onion, peppers and spring onion.
- Add the rest of the ingredients to the frying pan and fry for five minutes.
- Spread it over the fish, cut the lemon into quarters and serve it with the fish.

Serves: 4

Preparation time: 30 minutes

Chef tip: Jerk fish can go with anything like salad, pumpkin rice or fried dumpling; it is also a good dish for vegetarians.

PLANTAIN PORRIDGE

Ingredients:

- 2 plantains
- 1 pint of whole milk
- Spoon of cinnamon
- 1 tin of condensed milk
- Spoon of salt
- Spoon of vanilla essence
- Spoon of vanilla
- Spoon of nutmeg powder
- ½ cup of coconut milk
- 2 slices of hard dough bread
- 1 cup of water

Method:

- Put a medium sized pot on the stove, on gas mark 4 with the two cups of water and coconut milk, peel the plantains, cut them up small, place them into a blender with half of the whole milk and blend for 10 minutes.
- Place it into the pot with the water and coconut milk and leave to cook for 10 minutes. If it is too thick, you can add the rest of the whole milk and leave it to cook for a further 10 minutes.
- Add the rest of the ingredients except the bread and stir.
- Taste to see if it will need more salt.
- Leave to cook for five minutes
- Place in a serving bowl with the two slices of bread.

Serves: 4

Preparation time: 30 minutes

Chef tip: This is one of the best Jamaican porridges; other countries call this porridge by a different name.

JAMAICAN SKY JUICE

- 1 pint of water
- ½ cup of strawberry syrup
- 4 clear plastic bags
- 1 jug for mixing

Method:

- Pour the water into the jug with the syrup, mix it and taste it while mixing to see if it needs more water or more syrup.
- Pour half a cup of the juice into the bag and tie it.
- Place it into the freezer for 24 hours.

Serves: 4-5

Preparation time: 10 minutes

Chef tip: Suck Suck is a Jamaican tradition and most people will call it an ice lolly in England. Jamaican children will have it while going to school, with bulla cake and we call it Suck Suck.

FRIED CHICKEN

Ingredients:

- 1 kilo chicken
- 1 spoon of chicken seasoning
- 1 spoon of paprika
- 2 cups of plain flour
- 1 lemon
- 2 egg
- 1 cup of milk
- 1 litre of vegetable oil
- 1 spoon of all-purpose seasoning
- 1 spoon of coarse black pepper
- 1 spoon of meat seasoning
- 1 white onion, chopped up
- Pinch of fresh thyme, chopped up
- 1 spring onion chopped up
- Extra seasoning for the flour
- 1 spoon of paprika
- 1 spoon of chicken seasoning
- Spoon of all-purpose

Method:

- Wash the chicken with the lemon, place it into a big bowl, then add all of the seasoning except the flour, oil, egg and milk.
- Rub up the chicken and soak it for two hours, although 24 hours would be better.
- Beat the egg and milk together and pour it on the chicken in the bowl, rub it up, add the flour into another bowl
- Add all the flour seasoning and mix it up.
- Place a medium sized pot on the stove with the oil and heat it for 10 minutes, gas mark 6.
- You can also add an onion and fresh thyme to the oil.
- Once the oil is hot, place the chicken into the flour and rub the chicken, then shake the chicken and place it into the frying pan for 10 minutes.
- After 10 minutes check it with a fork. If it's not golden brown, leave it in the pan for another five minutes.
- Put it in a strainer and leave it for the oil to drain off for four minutes.

Serves: 4

Preparation time: 45 minutes

Chef tip: you can have this with, coconut rice, rice and peas, yam, banana, dumpling, vegetable rice.

HARD DOUGH BREAD

Ingredients:

- 2 cups of plain flour
- Pinch of salt
- 2 teaspoons of sugar
- 2 packs of yeast or 2 teaspoons of yeast
- 8 oz – 1 cup of water
- 1 bowl
- Spoon of shortening
- 1 teaspoon of vegetable oil
- Half a cup of extra flour

Method:

- Turn on the stove, gas mark 5.
- Place the water into a glass container and put it in a microwave for two minutes.
- Add the yeast, sugar, salt and shortening.
- Add the flour to the yeast, bit by bit, while mixing until it forms dough.
- The dough might be sticky so it's good to have extra flour, to sprinkle a little on the surface.
- Scrape off the dough on the surface and rub it up until it comes together.
- Get a clean bowl and use a food brush to dip in the oil and rub across the bowl.
- Put the dough into the bowl and leave it where it is warm.
- Get a damp kitchen towel or cling film and cover it for an hour.
- Once it's risen remove the towel, press down the dough, cover the dough again with the cling film or towel and leave it for a further 45 minutes.
- Remove the cling film and get a bread baking tray, place the dough in the tray and cover it again with the cling film for 20 minutes.
- Place in the oven and bake it for 30 minutes, gas mark 4.
- Remove from the oven and let it cool down for 20 minutes.

Serves: 10 people

Preparation time: 2 hours

Chef tip: once cool you can have this with butter, jam, soup, porridge.

SALT MACKEREL SERVED WITH BANANA AND DUMPLING

Ingredients:

- 1 kilo salt mackerel
- 1 spring onion, chopped up
- 1 large white onion, chopped up
- 1 small tomato, chopped up
- Pinch of fresh thyme
- ¼ of each mixed pepper chopped up
- 1 scotch bonnet pepper (cut a pinch)
- 2 teaspoon of ketchup
- Pinch of black pepper
- 1 small pot
- 4 cups of water
- 3 large spoons of oil

Method:

- Place a pot with the salt mackerel and water on the stove. Cook it for 15 minutes.
- Run the fish under cold water and remove the bone.
- Put it into a small bowl; place a medium size frying pan on the stove with the oil.
- Fry the rest of the ingredients, apart from the ketchup, for 10 minutes.
- Add the salt mackerel and cook it for eight minutes.
- Add the ketchup and leave it to simmer for another three minutes.
- Once simmered down you can serve it with dumpling and banana.

Serves: 4

Preparation time: 30 minutes

Chef tip: Salt mackerel is a Jamaican dish that goes with banana and dumpling. You can also add ackee or callaloo. It can go with plain rice, fried dumpling, festival dumpling and even hard dough bread.

Finale

CHEF RICARDO IS ON A MISSION TO PROMOTE CARIBBEAN CUISINE

Ricardo Campbell, more popularly known as Chef Ricardo, is not the kind of individual who waits for good things to happen; he makes them happen.

Not content with being able to prepare first-class Caribbean dishes, he has to share his passion for food with the world and has written two books on Caribbean cuisine which are available in stores and online.

Chef Ricardo was born in Jamaica. He grew up in and around the busy hotels and restaurants of Ocho Rios, one of Jamaica's main tourist resort areas.

As a young boy, he had a keen interest in cooking, spending a lot of time watching his elders cook many different dishes. He learnt a lot of trade secrets from his grandmother and his father who both loved cooking. His interest grew into a passion after leaving school.

He applied to be a kitchen assistant at a popular restaurant doing basic kitchen duties like preparing vegetables. Due to his eagerness he was given the opportunity to help prepare simple dishes like ackee and salt fish, rice and peas and brown stew chicken. After a short period he was making these dishes independently.

He told Jamaican Times: "I stayed in this restaurant for two years and moved on to work in one of the top hotel resorts where I excelled and progressed into becoming a range chef. My duties included cooking, being temperature control officer and ensuring that the presentation of the dishes was maintained to a high standard. I remained in this employment for ten years and obtained a chef's certificate."

In 2008 he moved to London to pursue further studies. He now works in the education sector as a chef at two institutions. He has more promotional projects in the pipeline and his work can be viewed at his website www.chefricardo.co.uk.

Chef Ricardo and his daughter, Kayla Campbell